The Easy & Enjoyable
MEMORY
Activity Book for Adults

By J.D. Kinnest

Filled with Fun Memory Activities, Easy Puzzles, Relaxing Brain Games and More

LOMIC BOOKS

The Easy & Enjoyable MEMORY
Activity Book for Adults

By J.D. Kinnest

ISBN: 978-1-988923-29-1
Published by Lomic Books
Kitchener, Ontario

Table of Contents

Table of Contents continued...

Introduction

Welcome to *The Easy & Enjoyable Memory Activity Book For Adults*. This book is filled with fun and relaxing ways to exercise your memory.

There is a great selection of activities in this book including: short-term memory games; long-term memory recall activities; as well as classic puzzles and brain games. Below you will find a description of some of the fun memory games and puzzles you will find in this book.

Short-term Memory Games

The short-term memory games in this book provide a relaxing way to exercise your brain. Some of the memory activities include:

- **Silly Sentences:** Have fun memorizing a silly sentence, and then, pick out the sentence from four different options.

- **Delightful Details**: In these puzzles, you memorize the details of a picture, then turn the page, and fill in a missing detail.

- **Backwards:** In this activity, write a fun sentence backwards to flex your short-term memory.

- **Terrific Lists:** You memorize a short list of six related items in this game, and then pick out the items from a word grid.

- **Particular Pictures:** In these games, you memorize three pictures; and then locate them on a page filled with pictures.

- **The Memory Challenge:** In this short-term memory game, you memorize a list of eight unrelated items, and then write down the items on the next page.

Long-term Memory Games

The long-term memory games in this book provide a fun way to energize your long-term recall.

- **Brainstorm:** Exercise your long-term recall by making a quick list of items related to a specific topic.

- **Begins With:** Use clues to recall words that begin with a specific letter and relate to the section's topic.

- **Lovely Memories:** In this activity, you write about a happy memory while recalling many interesting details.

- **Complete It:** In this long-term memory game, you fill in the missing word in a popular saying or phrase.

Classic Puzzles & Brain Games

There are many terrific puzzles and brain games in this book that provide a great variety of activities and extra mental exercise. The classic puzzles and brain games in this book include:

- **Word Searches**
- **Find the Differences**
- **Odd One Out**
- **Two of Kind**
- **Sudoku**
- **Pictures to Sayings**

Altogether, the combination of the short-term memory activities, long-term recall activities, and classic puzzles provides hours of mental exercise and entertainment.

Enjoy!

Going Out & Entertainment

Memory activities, puzzles, and brain games in this section include:

- ☑ **Delightful Details**
- ☑ **Begins With**
- ☑ **Picture to Saying**
- ☑ **Terrific Lists**
- ☑ **Lovely Memories**
- ☑ **Particular Pictures**
- ☑ **Word Search**
- ☑ **Rhyme Time**
- ☑ **Find the Differences**
- ☑ **Memory Challenge**

Begins with "P"

The answer to each clue begins with the letter "P" and relates to the section's theme of "Going Out & Entertainment."

1. A public procession down at street, may contain bands or floats.

2. A place for your main meal, when at a restaurant or at home.

3. Performed at a theater, but usually does not include singing.

4. A celebration that consists of a gathering of people.

5. A person who plays a traditional keyboard instrument.

6. Put your car in to a specific spot, before attending the theater.

7. Outdoor area of a restaurant, where you can eat your meal.

8. A great way to capture and remember a fun moment with friends.

Solution on page 136

Delightful Details

Take a moment to study the picture of an opera singer below. On the next page is an identical picture, that is missing two details. When you are ready, turn the page and fill in the missing details.

turn the page →

This puzzle continues from the previous page.

Delightful Details... continued

Have you studied the picture of the opera singer on the previous page? Great! Now draw in the two details that will make the image below identical to the image on the previous page.

Draw in the 2 missing details!

Solution on page 136

Terrific Lists... Out On The Town

In this memory game, the goal is to memorize the list provided, then turn the page, and circle the words you remember in the word grid.

Louise is going to the theater on Friday. To the right is a list of items she wants to buy for the outing. Once you have memorized Louise's list turn the page.

Louise's List

Skirt	tickets
lipstick	purse
blouse	shoes

turn the page

Dan is going to a music festival next week. To the right is a list of items he wants to buy so he can enjoy the outing. Once you have memorized Dan's list turn the page.

Dan's List

camera	beer
shorts	t-shirt
chips	comb

turn the page

This puzzle continues from the previous page.

Louise's List

Circle the items that you remember from Louise's list (found on the previous page) in the word grid.

shoes	lipstick	boots
sweater	bag	book
candy	wine	pants
blouse	suit	tickets
gum	tights	nuts
coat	skirt	jacket
scarf	brooch	purse

Dan's List

Circle the items that you remember from Dan's list (found on the previous page) in the word grid.

pants	juice	blanket
sweater	shorts	book
beer	phone	comb
hat	camera	belt
fruit	vest	cooler
shoes	pens	paper
t-shirt	watch	chips

Solution on page 136

FIND THE 5 DIFFERENCES

Find the 5 differences between the two pictures.

Solution on page 136   - 13 -

Lovely Memories...

Describe your favorite concert or musical performance that you attended in person — Which musician, band or singer was performing? Where was concert held? Did you like this location? Why? What songs did you most enjoy during the concert?

ADMISSION NO. 4015 5620 001

MUSIC
CONCERT

23.05
AT 20:00PM

AFTER SHOW

TICKET ADMIT ONE

PARTICULAR PICTURES
GOING OUT TO EAT

Take a look at, and memorize, the three restaurant items below. Then turn the page and pick out the three items that you memorized.

turn the page ➡

This puzzle continues from the previous page.

PARTICULAR PICTURES..... CONTINUED

Did you study the three items on the previous page? Great! Now circle the three restaurant items that you memorized.

Solution on page 136

RHYME TIME

In this activity, the goal is to write down words that rhyme with a specific "given" word. Take some time to think of as many words as you can, and write your answers on the lines provided.

List words that rhyme with "DANCE"

_____   _____   _____

_____   _____   _____

_____   _____   _____

_____   _____   _____

List words that rhyme with "BAR"

_____   _____   _____

_____   _____   _____

_____   _____   _____

_____   _____   _____

Solution on page 137

WORD SEARCH
GOING DANCING

In this puzzle, the goal is to find the words listed below, within the letter grid on the right. Each word is placed in either an across, diagonal or downward direction; and is spelled either forwards or backwards.

WORD LIST:

- BAND
- POLKA
- SWAY
- JITTERBUG
- ENERGY
- CLAP
- RHYTHM
- HULA
- MAMBO
- JIVE
- WALTZ

- BALLROOM
- STEP
- PARTNER
- DRESS
- TWIRL
- FANCY
- FUN
- SHOES
- CONGA
- TANGO
- LIFT

- FREESTYLE
- TIMING
- RUMBA
- FLOW
- CLOGGING
- MUSIC
- TAP
- SHUFFLE
- DISCO
- FOXTROT
- SEQUENCE

```
C M B C H R Q F Y C J P F F D E J I V E
L K B J O T E W R L J P N M F C W O L F
O K Q O A N X O W E X Q E T U J I E W J
G M I N E O G S P R E H R T I S S P F K
G K G W B O U A A T H S P T S R I H F J
I O X R G E Q F L I E Y T Q T Q X C E I
N Y I K G I Z N C Y S E T Y U D H F Q M
G U Q E C N E R O E R C F H L J Y D Y G
E W M A D I H U Q B V B R N M E I E A J
L L Y N Z I Q U U G B J A S A L U H W W
F F A N C Y E G H U I E C F S J Z B S K
F B R R Y N E T B O P Y Z R G E M Y R C
U J M Y C P F E V D P E M C K T R Q A I
H Y L E O I D K S G W X F I Z W T D W Z
S S F B L F M A M B O L O R V P V K N S
G A J P O L K A F M S T X Z E H U U B L
X D E G M K H T Z W B Y T B T N F H T F
C C H H L S M X U Y J O R O A Y T Y B A
G K H R C N H M G G V J O G P P P R L K
N S I R H Y G O Y W I Z T S X G M K A S
M W X O G O N K E M O O R L L A B A C P
T E Y R C F I R K S O F B F G S J W Y X
B Z E G I S M A B M U R U E Z T L A W P
V N V D L A I E D M D F J I O Q Z J L H
E A Y H B Q T D G W K T L D U M D E C D
```

SUDOKU FUN

In this entertaining brain game, the goal is to use the numbers 1 to 9 to fill in the grid below. To do so, you need follow three rules:

1. Each vertical row is filled with the numbers 1 to 9. You can use each number only once per row.

2. Each horizontal row is filled with the numbers 1 to 9. You can use each number only once per row.

3. Each 3 by 3 square, marked by the darker lines, is filled with the numbers 1 to 9, using each number once.

9		4		8	7			3
6	7	2	5	3		8	9	1
		5	2		9	7	6	
2	5			6	3	1	7	
	4	9	1		8	6		2
1	6		7		2	5	4	8
	8	1	3	4	6	9	2	
3			8	2		4	1	6
	2	6		7	1			5

Solution on page 137

The Memory Challenge

This activity is the most difficult of the short-term memory games. There is list of eight random words. The goal is to memorize the words, then turn the page, and write the words down in order.

The List:

1. Bird

2. Candle

3. Basket

4. Car

5. Ribbon

6. Table

7. Card

8. Tape

A HINT... (or how to make this challenge doable)

To help memorize a list of unrelated items, try using your imagination to make the items more memorable.

For example, if you are trying to remember the list:

> A. Dog
> B. Frisbee
> C. Boat

You could imagine..... A dog (Item A) is running along. The dog spots a frisbee (Item B), and picks it up with its mouth. The dog carries the frisbee to the beach and drops the frisbee in a boat (Item C).

Consider trying this approach with the list to the left.

turn the page

This puzzle continues from the previous page.

The Memory Challenge Continued

Write down the eight items you memorized from the previous page in the spaces provided.

1. _____

2. _____

3. _____

4. _____

5. _____

6. _____

7. _____

8. _____

Brain Game

PICTURE TO SAYING

In this brain game, the goal is to guess the saying depicted by the image below. Consider not only the pictures and/or words, but also how they are arranged.

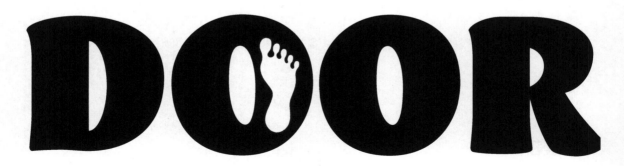

The Saying: _____

Solution on page 137

Lovely Forests & Wildlife

Memory activities, puzzles, and brain games in this section include:

- ☑ **Delightful Details**
- ☑ **Brainstorm**
- ☑ **Unscramble**
- ☑ **Silly Sentences**
- ☑ **Lovely Memories**
- ☑ **Particular Pictures**
- ☑ **Word Search**
- ☑ **Rhyme Time**
- ☑ **Lovely Memories**
- ☑ **Memory Challenge**

 **Brainstorm**

Make a list of different types of wild animals. How many can you think of?

1. _____
2. _____
3. _____
4. _____
5. _____
6. _____
7. _____
8. _____
9. _____
10. _____
11. _____
12. _____
13 _____
14. _____
15. _____
16. _____
17. _____
18. _____
19. _____
20. _____
21. _____
22. _____

UNSCRAMBLE TREES

Create words from the scrambled letters which relate to trees.

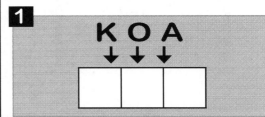

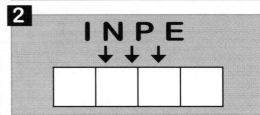

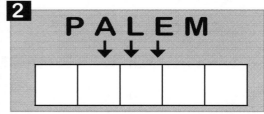

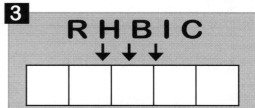

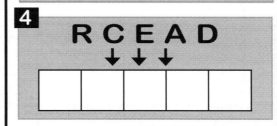

PARTICULAR PICTURES
DELIGHTFUL TREES

Take a look at, and memorize, the three trees below. Then turn the page and pick out the three trees that you memorized.

turn the page

This puzzle continues from the previous page.

PARTICULAR PICTURES..... CONTINUED

Did you study the three trees on the previous page? Great! Now circle the three trees that you memorized.

Solution on page 138   — 26 —

RHYME TIME

In this activity, the goal is to write down words that rhyme with the specific "given" word. Take some time to think of as many words as you can.

List words that rhyme with "BEAR"

_____ _____ _____
_____ _____ _____
_____ _____ _____
_____ _____ _____

List words that rhyme with "CROW"

_____ _____ _____
_____ _____ _____
_____ _____ _____
_____ _____ _____

Solution on page 138

FIND THE 5 DIFFERENCES

Find the 5 differences between the two pictures.

Solution on page 138

Lovely Memories...

Describe your favorite park or forest — Where is it located? What kind of trees and wildlife do you enjoy seeing when you visit? How does the park or forest smell? Write other details about the park or forest that you recall fondly.

WILD LIFE

NATIONAL PARK

WORD SEARCH
JUNGLE LIFE

In this puzzle, the goal is to find the words listed below, within the letter grid on the right. Each word is placed in either an across, diagonal or downward direction; and is spelled either forwards or backwards.

WORD LIST:

- ☐ LIZARD
- ☐ WATERFALL
- ☐ VEGETATION
- ☐ FUNGI
- ☐ DECAY
- ☐ WASP
- ☐ FLORA
- ☐ FERTILE
- ☐ LEOPARD
- ☐ FOX
- ☐ COUGAR

- ☐ BEETLE
- ☐ LEMUR
- ☐ ROOTS
- ☐ OWL
- ☐ SNAKE
- ☐ PARROT
- ☐ LEAVES
- ☐ EAGLE
- ☐ SHRUBS
- ☐ SPIDER
- ☐ LYNX

- ☐ VINES
- ☐ TREES
- ☐ MOTH
- ☐ AMAZON
- ☐ SOIL
- ☐ TIGER
- ☐ CANOPY
- ☐ BATS
- ☐ HYENA
- ☐ MONKEY
- ☐ GORILLA

```
O  L  P  E  S  T  O  O  R  M  D  V  R  L  I  W  A  S  P  M
S  F  G  W  K  S  U  E  L  P  P  G  V  F  K  A  E  G  P  L
N  Z  J  S  R  H  N  G  C  H  Y  E  N  A  R  A  P  E  B  E
A  V  U  P  M  C  A  N  O  P  Y  H  R  S  E  P  A  I  C  O
K  E  O  I  E  K  H  Z  L  X  N  E  E  L  Q  L  R  L  G  P
E  G  O  D  D  W  E  X  B  V  M  N  T  L  E  F  R  G  K  A
D  E  O  E  M  I  S  M  H  M  I  E  X  M  R  D  O  A  P  R
Y  T  P  R  W  O  V  I  N  V  E  U  U  H  K  H  T  I  N  D
T  A  R  S  I  C  C  E  C  B  P  R  I  T  Q  X  P  P  F  S
M  T  A  L  H  O  H  L  E  A  V  E  S  I  G  N  U  F  Y  C
N  I  V  M  K  R  B  S  C  Q  D  B  J  F  L  O  R  A  F  O
C  O  I  U  A  L  U  Q  T  R  R  M  D  R  T  J  B  T  V  U
K  N  Y  A  W  Z  M  B  K  S  J  E  J  C  M  B  W  F  D  G
A  E  J  T  U  I  O  S  S  M  H  H  U  R  D  L  M  O  E  A
S  G  G  G  A  R  K  N  O  U  Q  B  E  H  R  L  M  R  C  R
R  F  V  H  N  G  T  B  P  O  U  G  Y  Q  O  K  W  N  A  N
V  E  T  S  C  M  W  L  I  X  I  E  Z  O  L  F  L  Y  Y  M
P  R  M  A  V  F  U  M  I  T  O  G  Y  C  X  U  L  G  S  O
R  T  G  O  R  I  L  L  A  U  O  F  E  N  P  B  A  T  S  T
G  I  O  F  J  D  L  J  M  Q  R  Z  K  T  O  S  F  B  U  H
Q  L  W  J  R  G  F  S  E  J  D  F  N  C  D  T  R  E  G  K
O  E  L  A  E  B  E  D  W  Q  B  B  O  W  E  P  E  L  M  D
A  F  Z  H  X  E  V  X  Q  I  I  K  M  V  O  D  T  G  Q  C
M  I  W  L  R  Y  M  B  H  P  A  X  N  Y  L  K  A  A  Q  E
L  H  Z  T  F  P  S  A  A  G  T  V  X  P  O  B  W  E  T  E
```

SUDOKU FUN

In this entertaining brain game, the goal is to use the numbers 1 to 9 to fill in the grid below. To do so, you need follow three rules:

1. Each vertical row is filled with the numbers 1 to 9. You can use each number only once per row.

2. Each horizontal row is filled with the numbers 1 to 9. You can use each number only once per row.

3. Each 3 by 3 square, marked by the darker lines, is filled with the numbers 1 to 9, using each number once.

6	1		8	3	5	7	9	
5	8	2	9		7		6	1
		3	2	1	6	8	5	4
3	2			6	4	9	1	7
	6	1		8	2	4		5
4		5	1	9	3	2	8	
2	4	6	3		8		7	9
	5			7	1	6	2	3
	3	7	6	2	9	5		8

Silly Sentences...

Memorize the silly sentence below. Then see if you can pick it out from a selection of four similar sentences on the next page. Then repeat for the second silly sentence!

Sentence One:

"The giant giraffe eats lots of lovely leaves."

turn the page →

Sentence Two:

"Full forests are a happy home to beautiful birds."

turn the page →

This puzzle continues from the previous page.

SILLY SENTENCES..... CONTINUED

Sentence One:

Pick the silly sentence you memorized on the previous page from the four options below.

A) The giant giraffe eats lots of lovely leaves.

B) The enormous giraffe eats lots of lovely leaves.

C) The giant giraffe eats lots of tasty treats.

D) The giant elephant tastes lots of lovely leaves.

··

Sentence Two:

Pick the silly sentence you memorized on the previous page from the four options below.

A) Full forests are a happy hideout for beautiful bears.

B) Full jungles are a great home to beautiful birds.

C) Full forests are a happy home to beautiful birds.

D) Full forests are a happy hideout for beautiful birds.

Solution on page 139

Delightful Details

Study the picture of the toucan below. On the next page is an identical picture, that is missing two details. When you are ready, turn the page and fill in the missing details.

This puzzle continues from the previous page.

Delightful Details... continued

Have you studied the picture of the toucan on the previous page? Great! Now draw in the two details that will make the picture below identical to the image of the toucan on the previous page.

Draw in the 2 missing details!

Solution on page 139

Terrific Lists... Enjoy Wildlife

In these puzzles, the goal is to memorize the list, and then turn the page and circle the words you remember in the word grid.

Noah is going bird watching in a National Park. To the right is a list of birds he is studying and would like to spot on his trip. Once you have memorized Noah's list turn the page.

Noah's List

robin	stork
blue jay	lark
eagle	owl

turn the page

Jessica is going shopping for her camping trip in a wildlife preserve. To the right is a list of items she wants to buy for her trip. Once you have memorized Jessica's list turn the page.

Jessica's List

towel	blanket
matches	tent
hat	compass

turn the page

This puzzle continues from the previous page.

Noah's List

Circle the items that you remember from Noah's list (found on the previous page) in the word grid.

penguin	chicken	lark
quail	robin	parrot
stork	vulture	wren
warbler	turkey	blue jay
duck	swan	gull
pigeon	owl	cuckoo
eagle	sparrow	falcon

Jessica's List

Circle the items that you remember from Jessica's list (found on the previous page) in the word grid.

canoe	compass	sweater
towel	book	chair
netting	guide	boots
pan	blanket	games
cutlery	napkins	tent
hat	bag	cooler
crackers	cheese	matches

Solution on page 140

The Memory Challenge

This activity is the most difficult of the short-term memory games. There is list of eight random words. The goal is to memorize the words, then turn the page, and write the words down in order.

The List:

1. Roof

2. Grass

3. Spider

4. Flower

5. Ladder

6. Umbrella

7. Boots

8. Soap

A HINT... (or how to make this challenge doable)

To help memorize a list of unrelated items, try using your imagination to make the items more memorable.

For example, if you are trying to remember the list:

A. Dog
B. Frisbee
C. Boat

You could imagine..... A dog (Item A) is running along. The dog spots a frisbee (Item B), and picks it up with its mouth. The dog carries the frisbee to the beach and drops the frisbee in a boat (Item C).

Consider trying this approach with the list to the left.

turn the page

This puzzle continues from the previous page.

The Memory Challenge Continued

Write down the eight items you memorized from the previous page in the spaces provided.

1. _____

2. _____

3. _____

4. _____

5. _____

6. _____

7. _____

8. _____

Brain Game

WORDS UNDER CONSTRUCTION

▸ ▸ ▸ ▸ ▸ ▸ ▸ ▸ ▸ ▸ ▸ ▸ ▸ ▸ ▸ ▸ ▸ ▸ ▸ ▸

Write down words that you can form using the letters provided. You can use each letter once per word.

Letters   Words

C B A O L T

_____ _____

_____ _____

_____ _____

_____ _____

_____ _____

Solution on page 140

Solving Mysteries

Memory activities, puzzles, and brain games in this section include:

- ☑ Picture to Saying
- ☑ Backwards
- ☑ Rhyme Time
- ☑ Silly Sentences
- ☑ Lovely Memories
- ☑ Find the Differences
- ☑ Particular Pictures
- ☑ Entertaining Riddles
- ☑ Odd One Out
- ☑ Memory Challenge

RHYME TIME

In this activity, the goal is to write down words that rhyme with the specific "given" word. Take some time to think of as many words as you can.

List words that rhyme with "CLUE"

_____   _____   _____

_____   _____   _____

_____   _____   _____

_____   _____   _____

_____   _____   _____

List words that rhyme with "GUESS"

_____   _____   _____

_____   _____   _____

_____   _____   _____

_____   _____   _____

_____   _____   _____

Solution on page 140

PARTICULAR PICTURES
IT'S A MYSTERY

Take a look at, and memorize, the three items below. Then turn the page and pick out the three items that you memorized.

turn the page →

This puzzle continues from the previous page.

PARTICULAR PICTURES: IT'S A MYSTERY... CONTINUED

Did you study the three items on the previous page? Great! Now circle the items that you memorized.

Solution on page 141   - 44 -

Entertaining Riddles

Have fun trying to answer the fun riddles below. You can write your answer on the blank line provided.

Riddle One

I can keep the time, or be a way to carefully look at something. What am I?

Your Answer:

_____

Riddle Two

I am a useful piece of information, or an extra payment given for great service. What am I?

Your Answer:

_____

Riddle Three

I am a nice place to visit outdoors, and a way to place a vehicle in a garage. What am I?

Your Answer:

_____

Riddle Four

I am a short speech, and a nice way to prepare bread. What am I?

Your Answer:

_____

Solution on page 141

FIND THE 5 DIFFERENCES

Find the 5 differences between the two detectives.

Silly Sentences...

Memorize the silly sentence below. Then see if you can pick it out from a selection of four similar sentences on the next page. Then repeat for the second silly sentence!

Sentence One:

"Sarah solves a murky mystery
every Monday."

turn the page →

· ·

Sentence Two:

"The curious cop reads secret
sleuth books."

turn the page →

This puzzle continues from the previous page.

SILLY SENTENCES..... CONTINUED

Sentence One:

Pick the silly sentence you memorized on the previous page from the four options below.

A) Steven solves a murky mystery every Monday

B) Sarah solves a murky mystery every Monday.

C) Sarah solves a murky mystery every Sunday.

D) Steven solves a muddy mystery every Monday.

....

Sentence Two:

Pick the silly sentence you memorized on the previous page from the four options below.

A) The curious cop reads secret mystery magazines.

B) The curious teacher reads secret sleuth books.

C) The curious teacher writes secret sleuth books.

D) The curious cop reads secret sleuth books.

Solution on page 141

Lovely Memories...

Describe your favorite mystery movie or book — Who were the characters in the movie or book? What was the mystery? Who solved the mystery and how? Why do you enjoy this book or movie?

SPOT THE ODD ONE OUT

Find the picture that is different from the rest.

BACKWARDS SDRAWKCAB

In this activity, the goal is to write out the sentence backwards. Try to minimize the number of times you look at the original sentence to increase the level of difficulty of this memory challenge.

1.   I enjoy a great mystery.

Write it
backwards: _____

2.   How did you get here so fast?

Write it
backwards: _____

3.   Agatha Christie is my favorite author.

Write it
backwards: _____

4.   Sherlock Holmes is a great detective.

Write it
backwards: _____

Solution on page 142

SUDOKU FUN

In this entertaining brain game, the goal is to use the numbers 1 to 9 to fill in the grid below. To do so, you need follow three rules:

1. Each vertical row is filled with the numbers 1 to 9. You can use each number only once per row.

2. Each horizontal row is filled with the numbers 1 to 9. You can use each number only once per row.

3. Each 3 by 3 square, marked by the darker lines, is filled with the numbers 1 to 9, using each number once.

2	5	3	8		1		7	6
	4		2		3	5		
	6	8	5	7	4	3	1	2
		7	4	5	6	9	2	3
5	3	4		2	8			7
6			1	3		8	4	5
1	9		7	4		6	3	8
	8	2	6		5	7	9	4
4	7	6			9	2		

Solution on page 142

The Memory Challenge

This activity is the most difficult of the short-term memory games. There is list of eight random words. The goal is to memorize the words, then turn the page, and write the words down in order.

The List:

1. Necklace

2. Box

3. Rabbit

4. Plate

5. Pear

6. Table

7. Rug

8. Vase

A HINT... (or how to make this challenge doable)

To help memorize a list of unrelated items, try using your imagination to make the items more memorable.

For example, if you are trying to remember the list:

> A. Dog
> B. Frisbee
> C. Boat

You could imagine..... A dog (Item A) is running along. The dog spots a frisbee (Item B), and picks it up with its mouth. The dog carries the frisbee to the beach and drops the frisbee in a boat (Item C).

Consider trying this approach with the list to the left.

turn the page ➡

This puzzle continues from the previous page.

The Memory Challenge Continued

Write down the eight items you memorized from the previous page in the spaces provided.

1. _____   5. _____

2. _____   6. _____

3. _____   7. _____

4. _____   8. _____

Brain Game

PICTURE TO SAYING

Can you guess the saying depicted by the image below? Consider not only the pictures, but also how they are arranged.

The Saying: _____

Solution on page 142   - 54 -

The Joy of Cooking

Memory activities, puzzles, and brain games in this section include:

- ☑ Delightful Details
- ☑ Brainstorm
- ☑ Merry Matching
- ☑ Silly Sentences
- ☑ Lovely Memories
- ☑ Particular Pictures
- ☑ Word Search
- ☑ Complete It
- ☑ Two of a Kind
- ☑ Memory Challenge

Begins With "C"

The answer to each clue begins with the letter "C" and relates to the section's theme of "The Joy of Cooking."

1. A professional cook at a restaurant or on television.

_____

2. A bakery item often made for birthday's and other holidays.

_____

3. Describes brittle food like chips and fried chicken.

_____

4. A vegetable that is often thought to be good for the eyes.

_____

5. Small red-hot pepper, used to make a sauce with the same name.

_____

6. Common grain that is used to make cereal, often found in the 'ear.'

_____

7. A popular candy made from roasted cocoa beans.

_____

8. Dairy product that comes in many different forms and flavors.

_____

Solution on page 142   - 56 -

Delightful Details

Study the picture below. On the next page is an identical picture, that is missing two details. When you are ready, turn the page and fill in the missing details.

This puzzle continues from the previous page.

Delightful Details... continued

Have you studied the picture on the previous page? Great! Now draw in the two details that will make the image below identical to the image on the previous page.

Draw in the 2 missing details!

Solution on page 142

Silly Sentences...

Memorize the silly sentence below. Then see if you can pick it out from a selection of four similar sentences on the next page. Then repeat for the second silly sentence!

Sentence One:

"Super salad is the favorite dish
of healthy Hal."

turn the page ➜

· ·

Sentence Two:

"Betty bakes cute cupcakes
for Bob's birthday."

turn the page ➜

This puzzle continues from the previous page.

SILLY SENTENCES..... CONTINUED

Sentence One:

Pick the silly sentence you memorized on the previous page from the four options below.

A) Super salad is the delicious choice of healthy Hal.

B) Super soup is the favorite dish of healthy Hal.

C) Super salad is the favorite dish of healthy Ken.

D) Super salad is the favorite dish of healthy Hal.

....

Sentence Two:

Pick the silly sentence you memorized on the previous page from the four options below.

A) Betty bakes cute cupcakes for Bob's birthday.

B) Betty bakes tasty cake for Bob's birthday.

C) Doris bakes miniature cupcakes for Bob's birthday.

D) Betty bakes cute cookies for Dan's birthday.

Solution on page 142

PARTICULAR PICTURES
COOKING UTENSILS

Take a look at, and memorize, the three cooking tools below. Then turn the page and pick out the three items that you memorized.

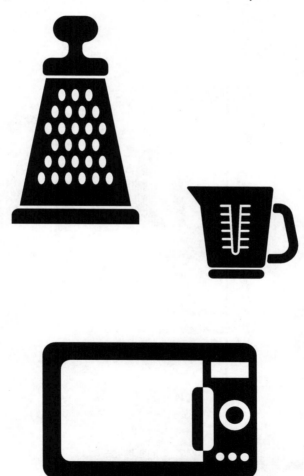

turn the page

This puzzle continues from the previous page.

PARTICULAR PICTURES..... CONTINUED

Did you study the three items on the previous page? Great! Now circle the three items that you memorized.

Solution on page 142

Lovely Memories...

Take some time to write about the meal you most like to cook or prepare. What are the ingredients? How do you prepare this meal? And what fond memories do your have about making or eating this meal?

WORD SEARCH
COOKING TECHNIQUES

In this puzzle, the goal is to find the words listed below, within the letter grid on the right. Each word is placed in either an across, diagonal or downward direction; and is spelled either forwards or backwards.

WORD LIST:

❏ HEAT	❏ WHISK	❏ BAKE
❏ DICE	❏ BROIL	❏ MIX
❏ FRY	❏ CHAR	❏ GLAZE
❏ SIMMER	❏ STEAM	❏ ZEST
❏ TASTE	❏ TOAST	❏ BASTE
❏ STEW	❏ SEASON	❏ PRESS
❏ BRAISE	❏ SEAR	❏ ROAST
❏ MINCE	❏ SLICE	❏ SAUTE
❏ WASH	❏ POACH	❏ CHOP
❏ ROLL	❏ MARINATE	❏ BOIL
❏ SCALD	❏ KNEAD	❏ PINCH

```
F  Z  T  P  R  Q  K  G  B  G  E  T  S  A  B  P  U  Q  V  T
S  L  H  K  H  B  M  W  D  E  L  P  R  G  N  P  H  U  N  K
L  Q  U  Y  B  F  O  J  M  Y  N  X  R  O  A  S  T  R  V  R
I  U  M  M  P  X  W  I  R  K  B  H  M  L  L  T  T  E  O  Z
C  H  R  Z  K  G  I  H  L  S  T  D  W  O  P  Y  K  L  I  F
E  U  D  K  E  K  A  B  E  R  B  O  D  Q  V  N  L  F  O  R
K  A  R  T  A  U  J  J  C  F  G  G  Q  B  E  W  Y  L  M  Y
S  I  N  Z  B  S  M  M  I  T  A  F  P  A  R  E  T  U  A  S
I  X  O  D  T  C  U  W  D  A  H  D  D  F  K  O  D  J  R  N
H  A  G  E  Z  C  C  E  O  K  A  S  P  I  W  T  I  O  L  Y
W  W  A  F  S  I  M  M  E  R  N  C  U  D  F  M  T  L  Q  F
X  M  F  H  J  Y  Z  S  H  S  V  A  M  R  W  P  O  H  C  I
Q  R  Q  C  B  K  F  E  X  Z  T  L  G  D  G  G  H  Z  P  U
T  A  A  J  E  V  G  X  S  X  I  D  T  J  Z  T  E  F  T  Y
C  E  M  E  G  J  O  W  R  T  U  K  Y  E  J  Y  S  M  I  X
N  J  K  I  S  Q  N  I  E  J  R  M  V  Q  P  G  J  W  F  E
V  L  X  Y  N  H  P  O  E  H  W  C  O  J  C  E  L  K  W  I
K  G  C  F  L  C  P  N  N  T  T  S  J  G  P  E  Z  A  L  G
E  S  W  W  C  A  E  T  Q  Q  A  Y  S  T  T  O  A  S  T  R
D  T  H  V  M  O  L  A  W  U  V  N  X  I  N  E  P  C  P  F
X  C  T  N  J  P  J  E  T  J  K  L  I  E  L  R  V  H  Z  B
K  H  N  S  B  O  T  H  O  I  S  K  X  R  E  S  C  Z  Q  U
Q  A  Z  I  H  S  X  N  O  S  A  E  S  S  A  N  W  A  S  H
K  R  V  P  S  H  A  T  K  P  X  A  S  P  I  M  G  O  N  T
X  L  U  S  B  R  A  I  S  E  Y  F  V  P  X  T  A  S  T  E
```

FIND TWO OF A KIND

Find the two aprons that are identical.

Solution on page 143

 **Brainstorm**

Make a list of different spices that are used for cooking. How many spices can you think of?

1. _____
2. _____
3. _____
4. _____
5. _____
6. _____
7. _____
8. _____
9. _____
10. _____
11. _____
12. _____
13 _____
14. _____
15. _____
16. _____
17. _____
18. _____
19. _____
20. _____
21. _____
22. _____

UNSCRAMBLE FRUITS

Create words from the scrambled letters that are kinds of fruits.

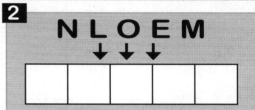

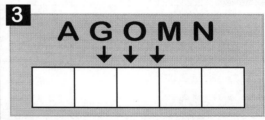

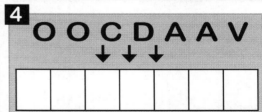

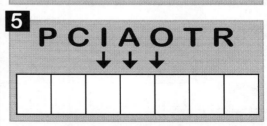

Solution on page 143

Complete It!
Famous Food Proverbs

In this memory game, the goal is to fill in the missing word in each food proverb.

1. Too many cooks _____ the broth.

2. Don't put all your _____ in one basket.

3. It's no use _____ over spilled milk.

4. You can't have your _____ and eat it too.

5. A watched pot never _____.

6. An _____ a day keeps the doctor away.

7. Don't bite off more than you can _____.

8. If life gives you _____, make lemonade.

9. Out of the frying _____ and into the fire.

10. The proof is in the _____.

Solution on page 143   - 68 -

Terrific Lists...Doing Groceries

In these puzzles, the goal is to memorize the list, and then turn the page and circle the words you remember in the word grid.

Sandy is going grocery shopping. To the right is a list of foods she wants to buy, so she is ready to prepare a meal tonight. Once you have memorized Sandy's list turn the page.

Sandy's List

lemon	lettuce
chicken	beans
pasta	milk

turn the page

Frank is planning to go grocery shopping. To the right is a list foods he want to buy for a party he is hosting. Once you have memorized Frank's list turn the page.

Frank's List

nachos	soda
salsa	crackers
wings	cheese

turn the page

This puzzle continues from the previous page.

Sandy's List

Circle the items that you remember from Sandy's list (found on the previous page) in the word grid.

milk	juice	lettuce
beef	bread	buns
chicken	butter	oil
pasta	carrots	corn
sugar	salt	lentils
flour	grapes	lemon
beans	onion	garlic

Frank's List

Circle the items that you remember from Frank's list (found on the previous page) in the word grid.

chips	pretzels	pecans
nachos	popcorn	cheese
cookies	fries	burgers
wings	tacos	dip
juice	beer	salsa
crackers	licorice	hot dogs
ice cream	soda	ketchup

Solution on page 144

SUDOKU FUN

In this entertaining brain game, the goal is to use the numbers 1 to 9 to fill in the grid below. To do so, you need follow three rules:

1. Each vertical row is filled with the numbers 1 to 9. You can use each number only once per row.

2. Each horizontal row is filled with the numbers 1 to 9. You can use each number only once per row.

3. Each 3 by 3 square, marked by the darker lines, is filled with the numbers 1 to 9, using each number once.

8		5	9	6		7	2	
	9	7			5	6	4	
6	4	2	8	1	7		5	9
7	1	8	2		3	4	9	6
	5			7	6	8		
	6	4	1	9		5	7	3
	2	6			1	9	3	5
5	7		6	3	2		8	
3		1	5	4	9	2	6	

Solution on page 144

MERRY MATCHING

How many times can you find this sequence in a straight line in the grid below?

NOTE: The sequence can be located vertically, diagonally, or horizontally in the grid. Also, the sequence may be displayed forwards or backwards.

The Memory Challenge

This activity is the most difficult of the short-term memory games. There is list of eight random words. The goal is to memorize the words, then turn the page, and write the words down in order.

The List:

1. Door

2. Fireplace

3. Jacket

4. Pail

5. Fish

6. Hose

7. Rock

8. Tree

A HINT... (or how to make this challenge doable)

To help memorize a list of unrelated items, try using your imagination to make the items more memorable.

For example, if you are trying to remember the list:

> A. Dog
> B. Frisbee
> C. Boat

You could imagine... A dog (Item A) is running along. The dog spots a frisbee (Item B), and picks it up with its mouth. The dog carries the frisbee to the beach and drops the frisbee in a boat (Item C).

Consider trying this approach with the list to the left.

turn the page →

This puzzle continues from the previous page.

The Memory Challenge Continued

Write down the eight items you memorized from the previous page in the spaces provided.

1. _____   5. _____

2. _____   6. _____

3. _____   7. _____

4. _____   8. _____

Brain Game

WORDS UNDER CONSTRUCTION

Write down words that you can form using the letters provided. You can use each letter once per word.

Letters   Words

Y H

E F

W A

_____   _____

_____   _____

_____   _____

_____   _____

_____   _____

Weather & Seasons

Memory activities, puzzles, and brain games in this section include:

- ☑ **Delightful Details**
- ☑ **Complete It**
- ☑ **Odd One Out**
- ☑ **Sudoku**
- ☑ **Lovely Memories**
- ☑ **Particular Pictures**
- ☑ **Word Search**
- ☑ **Find the Differences**
- ☑ **Silly Sentences**
- ☑ **Memory Challenge**

Complete It!
Fun Weather Sayings

In this memory game, the goal is to fill in the missing word in each fun weather saying.

1. Save for a _____ day.

2. Throw _____ to the wind.

3. The calm before the _____.

4. Every cloud has a _____ lining.

5. Take a rain _____.

6. A dark _____ on the horizon

7. There's nothing _____ under the sun.

8. Get your _____ out of the clouds!

9. Know which way the wind is _____.

10. Come rain or _____.

Solution on page 145

Delightful Details

1. Take a look at the picture to the right. On the next page is an identical picture, that is missing one detail. When you are ready, turn the page and fill in the missing detail.

turn the page

2. Take a look at the picture to the right. On the next page is an identical picture, that is missing one detail. When you are ready, turn the page and fill in the missing detail.

turn the page

This puzzle continues from the previous page.

1. Have you studied the picture on the previous page? Super! Now draw in the one detail that will make the image to the right, identical to the image on the previous page.

Draw in the 1 missing detail!

2. Have you studied the picture on the previous page? Super! Now draw in the one detail that will make the image to the right, identical to the image on the previous page.

Draw in the 1 missing detail!

Solution on page 145

FIND THE 5 DIFFERENCES

Find the 5 differences between the two pictures.

Solution on page 145

Lovely Memories...

Take some time to write about your favorite summer trip or vacation — Where did you go? What was the weather like when while you were there? What activities did you enjoy on this trip?

PARTICULAR PICTURES
LOTS OF WEATHER

Take a look at, and memorize, the three weather icons below. Then turn the page and pick out the three items that you memorized.

turn the page

This puzzle continues from the previous page.

PARTICULAR PICTURES..... CONTINUED

Did you study the three weather pictures on the previous page? Great! Now circle the three items that you memorized.

Silly Sentences...

Memorize the silly sentence below. Then see if you can pick it out from a selection of four similar sentences on the next page. Then repeat for the second silly sentence!

Sentence One:

> "Tom took too many photos of the twisty tornado."

turn the page ➤

· ·

Sentence Two:

> "Kim counts clouds outside her extra wide window."

turn the page ➤

This puzzle continues from the previous page.

SILLY SENTENCES..... CONTINUED

Sentence One:

Pick the silly sentence you memorized on the previous page from the four options below.

A) Tom took too many photos of the huffy hurricane.

B) Jerry took too many photos of the twisty tornado.

C) Terry took too few photos of the twisty tornado.

D) Tom took too many photos of the twisty tornado.

....

Sentence Two:

Pick the silly sentence you memorized on the previous page from the four options below.

A) Kim counts clouds outside her extra wide door.

B) Kim counts clouds outside her extra wide window.

C) Chloe counts clouds outside her extra wide window.

D) Kristina counts stars outside her extra wide window.

Solution on page 145

SPOT THE ODD ONE OUT

Find the picture that is different from the rest.

Solution on page 145

WORD SEARCH
SUMMER DAYS

In this puzzle, the goal is to find the words listed below, within the letter grid on the right. Each word is placed in either an across, diagonal or downward direction; and is spelled either forwards or backwards.

WORD LIST:

- [ ] TROPICAL
- [ ] HIKE
- [ ] HEAT
- [ ] TRAVEL
- [ ] VACATION
- [ ] RELAX
- [ ] SAILING
- [ ] OCEAN
- [ ] HAMMOCK
- [ ] OUTDOORS
- [ ] SNORKEL

- [ ] PICNIC
- [ ] DRESS
- [ ] HUMID
- [ ] CAMPING
- [ ] SWIM
- [ ] SHORTS
- [ ] HAT
- [ ] POOL
- [ ] SEASHELL
- [ ] RADIATE
- [ ] BIKING

- [ ] CLEAR
- [ ] BRIGHT
- [ ] LEISURE
- [ ] BEACH
- [ ] PARASOL
- [ ] FLOWERS
- [ ] T SHIRT
- [ ] SANDALS
- [ ] DAYLIGHT
- [ ] GOLF
- [ ] SUNNY

```
S  J  M  G  U  H  R  B  K  C  S  U  N  N  Y  M  A  Q  C  G
N  B  E  A  C  H  N  A  I  F  X  K  X  T  R  A  V  E  L  F
O  I  O  A  V  O  C  A  D  C  X  V  W  L  O  O  P  I  X  Y
R  A  T  H  G  I  R  B  E  I  A  D  H  H  J  K  L  G  P  W
K  L  B  V  H  K  N  S  I  C  A  M  J  G  W  W  Y  N  V  P
E  T  R  O  P  I  C  A  L  K  O  T  P  D  N  C  V  I  O  S
L  V  J  F  R  D  W  C  V  Z  O  O  E  I  T  H  A  L  W  R
O  I  S  F  I  I  M  G  O  L  F  H  U  O  N  T  C  I  A  P
V  W  C  R  C  M  O  S  K  P  V  B  E  T  M  G  A  A  U  I
U  I  G  P  C  U  B  C  U  S  E  M  V  S  D  C  T  S  S  C
L  D  Z  A  G  H  B  Y  L  W  L  Y  R  K  W  O  I  Y  U  N
M  E  K  R  T  E  N  O  T  I  S  D  Y  G  J  U  O  Z  G  I
S  B  I  A  N  J  C  U  C  M  Z  J  B  M  O  X  N  R  T  C
F  X  O  S  K  B  A  K  T  U  P  D  R  D  L  V  X  S  K
S  L  S  O  U  U  A  Z  T  W  A  E  K  I  H  R  P  L  I  V
M  B  O  L  W  R  T  H  G  I  L  Y  A  D  L  U  E  A  D  O
A  I  M  W  Q  A  E  I  F  U  V  C  T  E  U  N  F  S  M  I
L  K  M  C  E  C  X  L  I  K  R  L  T  A  E  H  J  G  S  V
S  I  M  O  U  R  L  B  O  C  E  N  Z  B  R  C  H  A  X  W
L  N  U  S  Z  E  S  Y  N  O  L  O  Q  S  A  R  L  T  O  T
A  G  Z  H  H  V  T  E  H  M  A  V  H  V  E  Y  J  B  S  R
D  W  T  S  D  F  R  G  Y  M  X  C  M  I  L  H  T  J  O  I
N  L  A  Y  M  R  O  T  Y  A  T  Q  D  F  C  T  W  U  D  H
A  E  Y  F  H  K  H  E  Z  H  A  K  W  M  Q  M  N  N  P  S
S  Y  E  D  J  G  S  C  J  T  H  N  V  Z  Z  Q  U  J  E  T
```

SUDOKU FUN

In this entertaining brain game, the goal is to use the numbers 1 to 9 to fill in the grid below. To do so, you need follow three rules:

1. Each vertical row is filled with the numbers 1 to 9. You can use each number only once per row.

2. Each horizontal row is filled with the numbers 1 to 9. You can use each number only once per row.

3. Each 3 by 3 square, marked by the darker lines, is filled with the numbers 1 to 9, using each number once.

		2	7	3	9	6	8	
9	6	8			4	3		7
4		7	6	8	5			1
	8	6	3	7		5	4	9
7	9	5	4		8	1		2
3			5	9	2	8	7	
6	7	9	8	2		4	1	5
	2			4	6	7	9	8
	4	1	9	5	7			3

The Memory Challenge

This activity is the most difficult of the short-term memory games. There is list of eight random words. The goal is to memorize the words, then turn the page, and write the words down in order.

The List:

1. Shelf

2. Curtain

3. Turtle

4. Bench

5. Pizza

6. Book

7. Leaf

8. Skirt

A HINT... (or how to make this challenge doable)

To help memorize a list of unrelated items, try using your imagination to make the items more memorable.

For example, if you are trying to remember the list:

> A. Dog
> B. Frisbee
> C. Boat

You could imagine..... A dog (Item A) is running along. The dog spots a Frisbee (Item B), and picks it up with its mouth. The dog carries the frisbee to the beach and drops the frisbee in a boat (Item C).

Consider trying this approach with the list to the left.

turn the page ➡

This puzzle continues from the previous page.

The Memory Challenge Continued

Write down the eight items you memorized from the previous page in the spaces provided.

1. _____

2. _____

3. _____

4. _____

5. _____

6. _____

7. _____

8. _____

Brain Game

WORDS UNDER CONSTRUCTION

Write down words that you can form using the letters provided. You can use each letter once per word.

Letters   Words

E
G
R
D
L
I

_____   _____
_____   _____
_____   _____
_____   _____
_____   _____
_____   _____

Solution on page 146   - 90 -

Word Cities & Urban Life

Memory activities, puzzles, and brain games in this section include:

- ☑ Begins With
- ☑ Backwards
- ☑ Unscramble
- ☑ Silly Sentences
- ☑ Lovely Memories
- ☑ Particular Pictures
- ☑ Word Search
- ☑ Terrific Lists
- ☑ Find the Differences
- ☑ Memory Challenge

Begins With "S"

The answer to each clue begins with the letter "S" and relates to the section's theme of "World Cities & Urban Life."

1. An underground train, that is often located in large cities.

_____

2. Very tall building, with many floors, that is found in big cities.

_____

3. Australia's most populated city that has a famous opera house.

_____

4. A very large structure where people go to see professional sports.

_____

5. The largest city/urban area in China, by population.

_____

6. A very common activity when at malls and stores.

_____

7. The capital city, and most populous city in Sweden.

_____

8. The outskirts of a city, that often has spaced out single family homes.

_____

Solution on page 146

PARTICULAR PICTURES
CITY STREET SIGNS

Take a look at, and memorize, the three city street signs below. Then turn the page and pick out the three items that you memorized.

This puzzle continues from the previous page.

PARTICULAR PICTURES..... CONTINUED

Did you study the three street signs on the previous page? Great! Now circle the three signs that you memorized.

Solution on page 147

 **Brainstorm**

Make a list of different cities or urban areas that you have visited. How many cities can you think of?

1. _____
2. _____
3. _____
4. _____
5. _____
6. _____
7. _____
8. _____
9. _____
10. _____
11. _____
12. _____
13. _____
14. _____
15. _____
16. _____
17. _____
18. _____
19. _____
20. _____
21. _____

UNSCRAMBLE CITY LIFE

Create words from the scrambled letters related to city life.

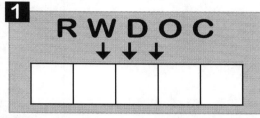

1 R W D O C

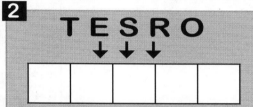

2 T E S R O

3 T H E O L

4 I S O Y N

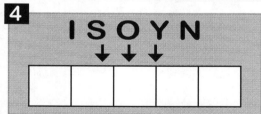

5 Y I H A H G W

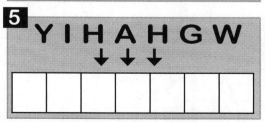

Solution on page 147

SPOT THE ODD ONE OUT

Find the picture that is different from the rest.

Solution on page 147

Terrific Lists... City Souvenirs

In these puzzles, the goal is to memorize the list, and then turn the page and circle the words you remember in the word grid.

Lisa is visiting New York City. To the right, is a list of souvenirs she wants to bring back for six of her friends. Once you have memorized Lisa's list turn the page.

Lisa's List

cup	map
postcard	stickers
bowl	pin

turn the page

Dale is visiting the Spanish city of Madrid. To the right, is a list of souvenirs he wants to bring back for six family members. Once you have memorized Dale's list turn the page.

Dale's List

vase	basket
sombrero	ring
scarf	journal

turn the page

This puzzle continues from the previous page.

Lisa's List

Circle the souvenirs that you remember from Lisa's list (found on the previous page) in the word grid.

collar	pin	cup
map	envelope	toy
t-shirt	paper	frame
flag	postcard	spoon
napkin	bottle	coin
gem	tree	stickers
bowl	glass	button

Dale's List

Circle the souvenirs that you remember from Dale's list (found on the previous page) in the word grid.

shell	basket	towel
scarf	laces	pencil
bracelet	vase	chain
plate	badge	tote
rug	journal	frame
sombrero	soap	statue
pillow	candle	ring

Solution on page 147

Lovely Memories...

Describe you favorite city. Write about some of the places in the city that you like to visit such as a favorite restaurant, park or museum. What special events or vacations have you enjoyed in this city?

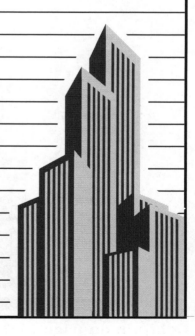

FIND THE 5 DIFFERENCES

Find the 5 differences between the two pictures.

Solution on page 147

Silly Sentences...

Memorize the silly sentence below. Then see if you can pick it out from a selection of four similar sentences on the next page. Then repeat for the second silly sentence!

Sentence One:

"Tanya takes the train to the merry museum."

turn the page ➜

· ·

Sentence Two:

"Wally waddles to the super subway station."

turn the page ➜

SILLY SENTENCES..... CONTINUED

Sentence One:

Pick the silly sentence you memorized on the previous page from the four options below.

A) Toby takes the taxi to the merry museum.

B) Tanya takes the taxi to the mindful museum.

C) Tanya takes the train to the merry museum.

D) Toby takes the train to the muddy museum.

....

Sentence Two:

Pick the silly sentence you memorized on the previous page from the four options below.

A) Wally walks to the great subway station.

B) Wally waddles to the super subway station.

C) Wendy walks to the silver subway station.

D) Wendy waddles to the super subway location.

Solution on page 147

SUDOKU FUN

In this entertaining brain game, the goal is to use the numbers 1 to 9 to fill in the grid below. To do so, you need follow three rules:

1. Each vertical row is filled with the numbers 1 to 9. You can use each number only once per row.

2. Each horizontal row is filled with the numbers 1 to 9. You can use each number only once per row.

3. Each 3 by 3 square, marked by the darker lines, is filled with the numbers 1 to 9, using each number once.

4			5	8	7		3	1
7	3	1	9		4	5	8	2
	5	8	2		1	7	4	
1	8	9		7	6	3		5
		3	1	9		6		8
6	2	7		5		4	1	9
3	1		7	2	9	8	6	
2	9		3			1	5	7
	7	4	6	1	5		9	3

Solution on page 148   - 103 -

WORD SEARCH
WORLD CITIES

In this puzzle, the goal is to find the words listed below, within the letter grid on the right. Each word is placed in either an across, diagonal or downward direction; and is spelled either forwards or backwards.

WORD LIST:

❏ MIAMI	❏ SEVILLE	❏ TORONTO
❏ BERLIN	❏ MADRID	❏ FLORENCE
❏ ZURICH	❏ BARCELONA	❏ CHICAGO
❏ CAMBRIDGE	❏ MUMBAI	❏ PRAGUE
❏ WASHINGTON	❏ LONDON	❏ DALLAS
❏ BRUSSELS	❏ TOKYO	❏ PARIS
❏ HONG KONG	❏ ROME	❏ ISTANBUL
❏ LAS VEGAS	❏ ATLANTA	❏ BEIJING
❏ OSLO	❏ LIMA	❏ CAIRO
❏ VENICE	❏ BRISTOL	❏ DUBAI
❏ MOSCOW	❏ VANCOUVER	❏ NEW YORK

```
F  E  O  R  I  A  C  V  B  R  I  S  T  O  L  S  D  O  I  V
O  B  Z  Y  B  L  A  P  W  S  O  B  P  U  N  U  O  A  C  A
H  Y  A  T  O  R  O  N  T  O  D  Y  D  A  B  A  B  W  N  N
F  P  X  R  L  O  L  I  M  A  D  P  J  A  R  Z  F  E  Z  C
I  M  B  L  C  V  Q  E  K  F  B  A  I  S  P  I  O  Z  V  O
I  O  N  D  C  E  P  R  A  G  U  E  L  V  B  U  S  E  Z  U
P  S  Q  E  A  X  L  R  S  H  E  S  Z  L  W  H  N  Z  W  V
V  C  T  H  W  P  E  O  P  E  L  K  A  X  A  I  K  N  T  E
S  O  G  A  J  Y  K  Y  N  Q  O  A  B  T  C  S  E  F  Q  R
A  W  L  Y  N  T  O  D  N  A  B  P  B  E  Q  T  P  K  D  S
G  S  J  I  I  B  E  R  K  N  W  R  N  E  J  I  C  U  S  E
E  E  V  M  Y  L  U  C  K  T  U  G  Z  X  R  O  M  Q  H  L
V  J  Y  N  E  H  R  L  N  S  N  L  U  E  M  L  W  U  K  O
S  Q  P  A  L  G  K  T  S  E  A  X  P  P  I  L  I  I  X  N
A  B  E  N  F  S  N  E  U  S  R  I  R  O  M  E  N  N  V  D
L  M  C  I  K  A  L  O  V  M  Y  O  X  L  D  A  C  N  C  O
V  I  A  U  S  S  T  E  K  E  P  U  L  Z  I  U  G  O  H  N
H  S  Q  D  X  Q  G  L  G  G  W  P  M  F  Y  D  Z  T  I  Q
G  E  C  T  R  A  B  D  A  F  N  C  P  F  W  S  G  G  C  P
U  V  T  O  S  I  I  B  M  N  C  O  I  A  H  O  N  N  A  F
H  I  C  M  S  R  D  I  B  A  T  A  H  C  Y  C  I  I  G  J
X  L  F  M  B  L  A  C  F  I  B  A  I  K  P  G  J  H  O  V
S  L  I  M  D  M  O  P  Y  M  U  R  O  Z  B  H  I  S  K  H
N  E  A  P  I  O  K  B  U  W  U  T  K  W  I  S  E  A  Y  A
P  C  F  J  N  U  V  M  J  Z  W  K  X  A  M  L  B  W  J  N
```

Solution on page 148

BACKWARDS   SDRAWKCAB

In this activity, the goal is to write out the sentence backwards. Try to minimize the number of times you look at the original sentence to increase the level of difficulty of this memory challenge.

1.   I enjoy the energy of the city.

Write it
backwards: _____

2.   The subway is a fast way to get around.

Write it
backwards: _____

3.   New York City has great museums.

Write it
backwards: _____

4.   The shops in London are terrific.

Write it
backwards: _____

Solution on page 148   - 106 -

The Memory Challenge

This activity is the most difficult of the short-term memory games. There is list of eight random words. The goal is to memorize the words, then turn the page, and write the words down in order.

The List:

1. Sweater

2. Chair

3. Squirrel

4. Blanket

5. Glasses

6. Television

7. Cookie

8. Pen

A HINT... (or how to make this challenge doable)

To help memorize a list of unrelated items, try using your imagination to make the items more memorable.

For example, if you are trying to remember the list:

    A. Dog
    B. Frisbee
    C. Boat

You could imagine..... A dog (Item A) is running along. The dog spots a frisbee (Item B), and picks it up with its mouth. The dog carries the frisbee to the beach and drops the frisbee in a boat (Item C).

Consider trying this approach with the list to the left.

turn the page →

This puzzle continues from the previous page.

The Memory Challenge Continued

Write down the eight items you memorized from the previous page in the spaces provided.

1. _____   5. _____

2. _____   6. _____

3. _____   7. _____

4. _____   8. _____

Brain Game

WORDS UNDER CONSTRUCTION

Write down words that you can form using the letters provided. You can use each letter once per word.

Letters   ## Words

R
P
V   I
E   T

_____   _____

_____   _____

_____   _____

_____   _____

_____   _____

_____   _____

Hobbies & Games

Memory activities, puzzles, and brain games in this section include:

- ☑ **Begins With**
- ☑ **Two of a Kind**
- ☑ **Brainstorm**
- ☑ **Delightful Details**
- ☑ **Terrific Lists**

- ☑ **Word Search**
- ☑ **Particular Pictures**
- ☑ **Rhyme Time**
- ☑ **Picture to Saying**
- ☑ **Memory Challenge**

SPOT THE ODD ONE OUT

Find the picture that is different from the rest.

Begins With "B"

The answer to each clue begins with the letter "B" and relates to the section's theme of "Hobbies & Games."

1. Popular hobby that has people looking to the sky with binoculars.

_____

2. Monopoly, Clue and Trouble are examples of this kind of game.

_____

3. It provides a relaxing way to pass time, and usually includes a plot.

_____

4. Entertaining game that uses a particularly heavy ball.

_____

5. Enjoyable and tasty past-time that requires consistent heat.

_____

6. A hobby whose end result is primarily a golden fluid.

_____

7. A game where the goal is to put the ball in the net again and again.

_____

8. A game that is played using cues and a custom table.

_____

Solution on page 149

Brainstorm

Make a list of items that people often collect as a hobby. How many different items can you think of?

1. _____
2. _____
3. _____
4. _____
5. _____
6. _____
7. _____
8. _____
9. _____
10. _____
11. _____
12. _____
13 _____
14. _____
15. _____
16. _____
17. _____
18. _____
19. _____
20. _____
21. _____

UNSCRAMBLE POTTERY

Create words from the scrambled letters related to pottery.

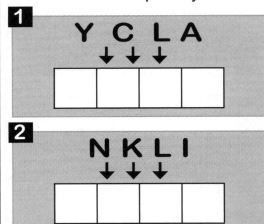

1 Y C L A

2 N K L I

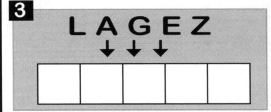

3 L A G E Z

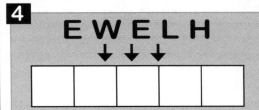

4 E W E L H

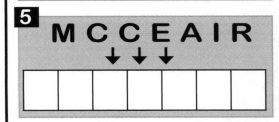

5 M C C E A I R

PARTICULAR PICTURES
STAMP COLLECTING

Take a look at, and memorize, the three stamps below. Then turn the page and pick out the three stamps that you memorized.

turn the page

This puzzle continues from the previous page.

PARTICULAR PICTURES: STAMP COLLECTING... CONTINUED

Did you study the three stamps on the previous page? Great! Now circle the three stamps that you memorized.

Solution on page 149

Lovely Memories...

Take some time to write about your favorite hobby — What is you favorite hobby and why? When do you like to work on your hobby? How did you start participating in this hobby? And why is this hobby meaningful to you?

BACKWARDS SDRAWKCAB

In this activity, the goal is to write out the sentence backwards. Try to minimize the number of times you look at the original sentence to increase the level of difficulty of this memory challenge.

1. Knitting is relaxing for Bridget.

Write it
backwards: ———————————————————

2. George painted a landscape yesterday.

Write it
backwards: ———————————————————

3. Karen sculpts beautiful clay pots.

Write it
backwards: ———————————————————

4. Quilting is fun to do in groups.

Write it
backwards: ———————————————————

Solution on page 149 - 116 -

Delightful Details

Study the picture of the golfer below. On the next page is an identical picture, that is missing two details. When you are ready, turn the page and fill in the missing details.

turn the page

This puzzle continues from the previous page.

Delightful Details... continued

Have you studied the picture of the golfer on the previous page? Great! Now draw in the two details that will make the image below identical to the image on the previous page.

Draw in the 2 missing details!

Solution on page 149

RHYME TIME

In this activity, the goal is to write down words that rhyme with a specific "given" word. Take some time to think of as many words as you can, and write your answers on the lines provided.

List words that rhyme with "GAME"

_____ _____ _____

_____ _____ _____

_____ _____ _____

_____ _____ _____

List words that rhyme with "READ"

_____ _____ _____

_____ _____ _____

_____ _____ _____

_____ _____ _____

Solution on page 150

WORD SEARCH
COIN COLLECTING

In this puzzle, the goal is to find the words listed below, within the letter grid on the right. Each word is placed in either an across, diagonal or downward direction; and is spelled either forwards or backwards.

WORD LIST:

❑ PRISTINE	❑ DISPLAY	❑ NICKLE
❑ CURRENCY	❑ METAL	❑ YEAR
❑ HISTORIC	❑ BINDER	❑ PENNY
❑ SHILLING	❑ SILVER	❑ BOX
❑ MINT	❑ COPPER	❑ QUARTER
❑ ZINC	❑ USED	❑ FINISH
❑ BUY	❑ ARTISTIC	❑ MONEY
❑ VALUE	❑ TRADE	❑ AUCTION
❑ ALBUM	❑ CHANGE	❑ DOLLAR
❑ DESIGN	❑ DIME	❑ TUBES
❑ PENCE	❑ GOLD	❑ BRONZE

```
I  R  E  D  N  I  B  R  T  T  S  Q  G  W  C  S  N  J  T  U
J  P  L  Y  J  S  V  T  N  L  C  O  P  P  E  R  T  S  M  O
J  H  C  V  J  U  U  H  K  E  P  G  A  M  V  T  Q  X  J  R
I  D  L  G  H  I  S  T  O  R  I  C  U  U  T  G  G  Z  P  A
S  Y  K  B  U  Y  A  R  O  Z  E  B  L  X  C  J  N  R  T  L
D  P  N  T  A  G  D  I  S  P  L  A  Y  F  L  T  I  N  W  L
P  W  A  N  P  H  E  I  Y  A  C  Y  Z  W  T  S  I  V  C  O
A  V  C  O  E  E  L  J  A  E  I  L  P  Q  T  V  S  O  B  D
G  Y  B  E  D  P  K  P  T  S  P  U  H  I  U  W  P  J  N  Q
S  H  R  B  L  K  C  A  P  N  Z  I  N  C  T  B  C  O  U  Y
I  P  O  H  E  W  I  K  I  D  M  E  W  P  O  M  U  A  Y  I
L  D  N  M  X  E  N  E  C  U  N  S  K  F  F  R  R  Z  G  N
V  M  Z  B  D  M  L  G  H  I  O  A  M  V  J  T  R  O  G  G
E  Z  E  A  S  I  Q  N  O  Q  T  F  S  S  E  J  E  G  U  I
R  Z  R  D  V  W  M  A  O  B  Y  S  U  R  F  K  N  M  E  S
Y  T  L  P  E  X  W  H  Z  Y  M  J  I  V  X  K  C  O  I  E
E  J  G  P  Y  S  E  C  P  V  H  C  F  T  W  J  Y  B  B  D
F  M  S  S  Y  D  U  G  Y  R  C  B  M  J  R  G  D  P  I  W
Y  Y  T  M  L  D  N  U  L  Y  O  Y  L  R  L  A  W  M  K  T
T  G  Z  O  Z  I  G  P  V  X  T  P  J  A  M  A  E  R  V  Y
U  K  G  O  L  P  Y  F  E  M  U  Y  V  Q  L  E  T  A  B  C
B  T  J  L  L  P  N  N  Z  I  M  E  V  W  X  T  S  E  I  Y
E  S  I  F  I  N  I  S  H  N  D  N  E  M  I  D  V  Y  M  C
S  H  C  L  P  A  Q  O  F  T  Z  O  H  P  S  V  A  L  U  E
S  J  C  W  Q  K  Z  R  D  E  V  M  L  L  O  P  E  N  C  E
```

FIND TWO OF A KIND

Find the two pictures that are identical.

Solution on page 150

Terrific Lists... Hello Hobbies

In these puzzles, the goal is to memorize the list, and then turn the page and circle the items you remember in the word grid.

Kelly is going shopping for art supplies, to create a painting. To the right is a list of items she wants to buy. Once you have memorized Kelly's list, turn the page.

Kelly's List

canvas	apron
brush	pencil
paint	easel

turn the page

Justin is going to buy some items for his model train project. To the right is a list of things he wants to buy. Once you have memorized Justin's list, turn the page.

Justin's List

rail	wire
logs	boxcar
fence	engine

turn the page

This puzzle continues from the previous page.

Kelly's List

Circle the items that you remember from Kelly's list (found on the previous page) in the word grid.

easel	paper	pencil
pens	markers	palette
brush	panel	fabric
bowl	box	canvas
towel	spoon	knife
tape	chair	tote
stickers	apron	paint

Justin's List

Circle the items that you remember from Justin's list (found on the previous page) in the word grid.

glue	bushes	bumper
crane	rail	engine
wire	coupler	deck
fence	gear	switch
resistor	paint	boxcar
tree	cabin	bench
logs	caboose	combine

Solution on page 150

The Memory Challenge

This activity is the most difficult of the short-term memory games. There is list of eight random words. The goal is to memorize the words, then turn the page, and write the words down in order.

The List:

1. Book

2. Socks

3. Duck

4. Mirror

5. Fence

6. Lamp

7. Pool

8. Shovel

A HINT... (or how to make this challenge doable)

To help memorize a list of unrelated items, try using your imagination to make the items more memorable.

For example, if you are trying to remember the list:

A. Dog
B. Frisbee
C. Boat

You could imagine..... A dog (Item A) is running along. The dog spots a frisbee (Item B), and picks it up with its mouth. The dog carries the frisbee to the beach and drops the frisbee in a boat (Item C).

Consider trying this approach with the list to the left.

turn the page ➡

This puzzle continues from the previous page.

The Memory Challenge Continued

Write the eight items you memorized from the previous page in the spaces provided.

1. _____   5. _____

2. _____   6. _____

3. _____   7. _____

4. _____   8. _____

Brain Game

PICTURE TO SAYING

Can you guess the saying depicted by the image to the right? Consider not only the pictures, but also how they are arranged.

The Saying: _____

Solution on page 151

Bonus Section

In this section, you will find the following memory activities and puzzles:

☑ **Delightful Details**   ☑ **Complete It!**

☑ **Brainstorm**   ☑ **Word Search**

☑ **Unscramble**   ☑ **Find the Differences**

Brainstorm

Make a list of different dog breeds. How many different dog breeds can you think of?

1. _____
2. _____
3. _____
4. _____
5. _____
6. _____
7. _____
8. _____
9. _____
10. _____
11. _____
12. _____
13 _____
14. _____
15. _____
16. _____
17. _____
18. _____
19. _____
20. _____
21. _____
22. _____

UNSCRAMBLE DESSERT

Create words from the scrambled letters related to dessert.

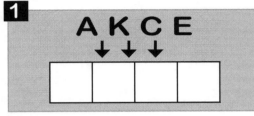

1 A K C E

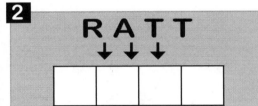

2 R A T T

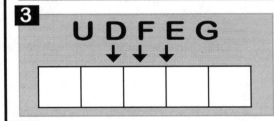

3 U D F E G

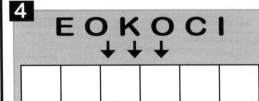

4 E O K O C I

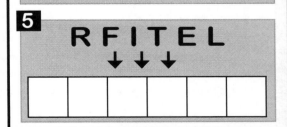

5 R F I T E L

Delightful Details

Take a moment to study the picture of the lady walking a dog below. On the next page is an identical picture, that is missing two details. When you are ready, turn the page and fill in the missing details.

turn the page

This puzzle continues from the previous page.

Delightful Details... continued

Have you studied the picture of the lady walking a dog on the previous page? Great! Now draw in the two details that will make the image below identical to the image on the previous page.

Draw in the 2 missing details!

Solution on page 151

Complete It!
Fun Positive Sayings

In this memory game, the goal is to fill in the missing word in each positive saying.

1. If at first you don't succeed, try, _____ again.

2. You _____ what you sow.

3. Many hands make _____ work.

4. Honesty is the best _____.

5. There is no time like the _____.

6. Where there's a _____ there's a way.

7. Great oaks from little _____ grow.

8. What goes around, comes _____.

9. Fortune favors the _____.

10. Alls _____ that ends well.

Solution on page 151   - 131 -

WORD SEARCH
MUSICAL INSTRUMENTS

In this puzzle, the goal is to find the words listed below, within the letter grid on the right. Each word is placed in either an across, diagonal or downward direction; and is spelled either forwards or backwards.

WORD LIST:

- VIOLIN
- GUITAR
- TRUMPET
- CYMBAL
- BELL
- PICCOLO
- CELLO
- HARP
- WHISTLE
- BAGPIPE
- GONG
- FLUTE
- DRUM
- ORGAN
- VIOLA
- BONGO
- CLARINET
- PIANO
- TUBA
- ZITHER
- FIDDLE
- OBOE
- TROMBONE
- XYLOPHONE
- ACCORDION
- MARACAS
- GLOCKENSPIEL
- SAXOPHONE
- MANDOLIN
- TRIANGLE
- CLAVICHORD
- TAMBOURINE
- HARMONICA

```
P R L H N Q N O X E L T S I H W O T C E
I C Y M N W Q Q T Q B V A T A P K V V Y R
A P L F X Y L O P H O N E A R F N R W Y
N J M A A L H C S H R E C F P Y C O H N
O M A S R O B O E S K N O I D R O C C A
P V N G A I F Q M L F N B G G H W A Z D
I G D D U X N H M W L B O O T U B A W U
A A O O R V O E H R F O N E M C A X R U
B R L L W U K P T J C G G A M B B L N H
E C I L N F M O H N I L O I V I G L F V
L F N P R T Y X E O Z M C J L C G M C B
D H D P I X I Q R A N M A R A C A S X G
D K E N O B M O R T H E F M A E V U L L
I Z U T E L Z I T H E R E C R V W O X E
F T A M B O U R I N E C I P I C C O L O
D L W N T R U M P E T N Z Z G K V J W L
R U E B I R G M A W O G M V E Z W T V R
O J C H O W R M U M E Y I N G P F R I E
H A H T K D W K R T L O S E J J G I R P
C L U O T J R A U V L P M U X F B A J I
I A U U A F H L W A I Q V Q N E D N A P
V B K Q F B F G N E O I Y A L E J G M G
A M W N Y W D O L R Y H G L P Y N L H A
L Y R A T I U G O T N R A A M V I E E B
C C F M F J D B D B O A I G T A O R S Z
```

FIND THE 5 DIFFERENCES

Find the 5 differences between the two pictures.

Solution on page 152   - 134 -

ANSWERS

Answers

Page 8: Begins With 'P'

1. Parade
2. Plate
3. Play
4. Party
5. Pianist
6. Park
7. Patio
8. Photo

Pages 9-10: Details

Pages 11-12: Louise's List

shoes *(circled)* lipstick *(circled)* boots
sweater bag book
candy wine pants
blouse *(circled)* suit tickets *(circled)*
gum tights nuts
coat Skirt *(circled)* jacket
scarf brooch purse *(circled)*

Pages 11-12: Dan's List

pants juice blanket
sweater shorts *(circled)* book
beer *(circled)* phone comb *(circled)*
hat camera *(circled)* belt
fruit vest cooler
shoes pens paper
t-shirt *(circled)* watch chips *(circled)*

Page 13: Find the Differences

Pages 15-16: Particular Pictures

Page 17: Rhyme Time

Rhymes with "Dance"
Chance, glance, lance, finance, France, stance, advance, romance, freelance, circumstance. *Other answers are possible.*

Rhymes with "Bar"
Char, far, tar, jar, scar, star, spar, czar, are, bazaar, seminar, par, jaguar, guitar, car, radar, cigar. *Other answers are possible.*

Pages 18-19: Word Search, Dancing

Page 20: Sudoku

9	1	4	6	8	7	2	5	3
6	7	2	5	3	4	8	9	1
8	3	5	2	1	9	7	6	4
2	5	8	4	6	3	1	7	9
7	4	9	1	5	8	6	3	2
1	6	3	7	9	2	5	4	8
5	8	1	3	4	6	9	2	7
3	9	7	8	2	5	4	1	6
4	2	6	9	7	1	3	8	5

Pages 21-22: Memory Challenge

1. Bird
2. Candle
3. Basket
4. Car
5. Ribbon
6. Table
7. Card
8. Tape

Page 22: Picture to Saying

Get your foot in the door.

Answers

Page 24: Brainstorm, Wild Animals

Coyote, skunk, lion, fox, deer, raccoon, squirrel, giraffe, elk, beaver, bear, monkey, warthog, gorilla, zebra, chipmunk, rhinoceros, panther, kangaroo, elephant, koala. *Many other answers are possible.*

Page 24: Unscramble, Trees

1. Oak   2. Pine   3. Maple   4. Birch   5. Cedar

Pages 25-26: Particular Pictures

Page 28: Find the Differences

Page 27: Rhyme Time

Rhymes with "Bear"

Share, air, fair, blare, flare, care, chair, pear, mare, stair, stare, square, hair, glare, wear, square, there, compare. *Other answers are possible.*

Rhymes with "Crow"

Flow, glow, blow, show, row, mow, slow, banjo, grow, throw, low, beau, toe, know, go, below, no, sew, although. *Other answers are possible.*

Pages 33-34: Sentences

Sentence One:

A) The giant giraffe eats lots of lovely leaves.

Sentence Two:

C) Full forests are a happy home to beautiful birds.

Pages 30-31: Word Search, Jungle

```
O L P E S T O O R M D V R L I W A S P M
S F G W K S U E L P P G V F K A E G P L
N Z J S R H N G C H Y E N A R A P E B E
A V U P M C A N O P Y H R S E P A I C O
K E O I E K H Z L X N E E L Q L R L G P
E G O D D W E X B V M N T L E F R G K A
D E O E M I S M H M I E X M R D O A P R
Y T P R W O V I N V E U U H K H T I N D
T A R S I C C E C B P R I T Q X P P F S
M T A L H O H L E A V E S I G N U F Y C
N I V M K R B S C Q D B J F L O R A F O
C O I U A L U Q T R R M D R T J B T V U
K N Y A W Z M B K S J E J C M B W F D G
A E J T U I O S S M H H U R D L M O E A
S G G G A R K N O U Q B E H R L M R C R
R F V H N G T B P O U G Y Q O K W N A N
V E T S C M W L I X I E Z O L F L Y A M
P R M A V F U M I T O G Y C X U L G S O
R T G O R I L L A U O F E N P B A T S T
G I O F J D L J M Q R Z K T O S F B U H
Q L W J R G F S E J D F N C D T R E G K
O E L A E B E D W Q B B O W E P E L M D
A F Z H X E V X Q I I K M V O D T G Q C
M I W L R Y M B H P A X N Y L K A A Q E
L H Z T F P S A A G T V X P O B W E T E
```

Pages 35-36: Details

Page 32: Sudoku

6	1	4	8	3	5	7	9	2
5	8	2	9	4	7	3	6	1
7	9	3	2	1	6	8	5	4
3	2	8	5	6	4	9	1	7
9	6	1	7	8	2	4	3	5
4	7	5	1	9	3	2	8	6
2	4	6	3	5	8	1	7	9
8	5	9	4	7	1	6	2	3
1	3	7	6	2	9	5	4	8

Pages 37-38: Noah's List

penguin	chicken	(lark)
quail	(robin)	parrot
(stork)	vulture	wren
warbler	turkey	(blue jay)
duck	swan	gull
pigeon	(owl)	cuckoo
(eagle)	sparrow	falcon

Pages 37-38: Jessica's List

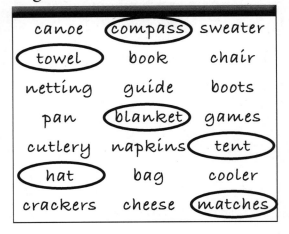

canoe	(compass)	sweater
(towel)	book	chair
netting	guide	boots
pan	(blanket)	games
cutlery	napkins	(tent)
(hat)	bag	cooler
crackers	cheese	(matches)

Pages 39-40: Challenge

1. Roof	5. Ladder
2. Grass	6. Umbrella
3. Spider	7. Boots
4. Flower	8. Soap

Page 40: Letters C, B, A, O, L, T

cobalt	colt	lot
bloat	bat	cab
taco	act	lab
cola	boa	bot
boat	oat	cob
blot	tab	at
coal	lob	to
coat	tao	*Other*
talc	alt	*words are*
alto	cat	*possible.*

Page 42: Rhyme Time

Rhymes with "Clue"

Blue, shoe, true, new, flu, glue, slew, chew, dew, brew, cue, flew, you, two, shoo, who, hue, due, crew, screw, drew, threw, through. *Other answers are possible.*

Rhymes with "Guess"

Dress, bless, mess, chess, cress, less, press, yes, stress, progress, impress, success, depress, impress, possess, tress. *Other answers are possible.*

Page 45: Riddles

1. Watch   3. Park
2. Tip   4. Toast

Page 46: Find the Differences

Pages 47-48: Sentences

Sentence One:

B) Sarah solves a murky mystery every Monday.

Sentence Two:

D) The curious cop reads secret sleuth books.

Pages 43-44: Particular Pictures

Page 50: Odd One Out

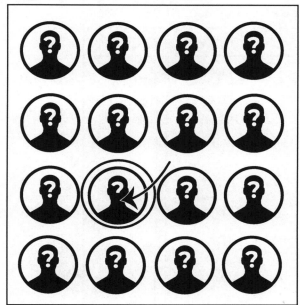

Page 51: Backwards

1. .yretsym taerg a yojne I
2. ?tsaf os ereh teg uoy did woH
3. .rohtua etirovaf ym si eitsirhC ahtagA
4. .evitceted taerg a si semloH kcolrehS

Pages 53-54: Challenge

1. Necklace
2. Box
3. Rabbit
4. Plate
5. Pear
6. Table
7. Rug
8. Vase

Page 54: Picture to Saying

Read between the lines.

Page 56: 'C'

1. Chef
2. Cake
3. Crispy
4. Carrot
5. Chili
6. Corn
7. Chocolate
8. Cheese

Pages 57-58: Details

Page 52: Sudoku

2	5	3	8	9	1	4	7	6
7	4	1	2	6	3	5	8	9
9	6	8	5	7	4	3	1	2
8	1	7	4	5	6	9	2	3
5	3	4	9	2	8	1	6	7
6	2	9	1	3	7	8	4	5
1	9	5	7	4	2	6	3	8
3	8	2	6	1	5	7	9	4
4	7	6	3	8	9	2	5	1

Pages 59-60: Sentences

Sentence One:
D) Super salad is the favorite dish of healthy Hal.

Sentence Two:
A) Betty bakes cute cupcakes for Bob's birthday.

Pages 61-62: Particular Pictures

Page 66: Two of a Kind

Page 67: Brainstorm

Ginger, cinnamon, turmeric, nutmeg, fennel, cumin, saffron, caraway seed, onion powder, pumpkin spice, chili pepper, paprika, peppercorn, basil, thyme, vanilla. *Many other answers are possible.*

Page 67: Unscramble

1. Apple
2. Lemon
3. Mango
4. Avocado
5. Apricot

Page 68: Complete It!

1. Spoil
2. Eggs
3. Crying
4. Cake
5. Boils
6. Apple
7. Chew
8. Lemons
9. Pan
10. Pudding

Pages 64-65: Word Search, Cooking

Answers

Pages 69-70: Sandy

(milk)   juice   (lettuce)
beef   bread   buns
(chicken)   butter   oil
(pasta)   carrots   corn
sugar   salt   lentils
flour   grapes   (lemon)
(beans)   onion   garlic

Pages 69-70: Frank

chips   pretzels   pecans
(nachos)   popcorn   (cheese)
cookies   fries   burgers
(wings)   tacos   dip
juice   beer   (salsa)
(crackers)   licorice   hot dogs
ice cream   (soda)   ketchup

Page 71: Sudoku

8	3	5	9	6	4	7	2	1
1	9	7	3	2	5	6	4	8
6	4	2	8	1	7	3	5	9
7	1	8	2	5	3	4	9	6
9	5	3	4	7	6	8	1	2
2	6	4	1	9	8	5	7	3
4	2	6	7	8	1	9	3	5
5	7	9	6	3	2	1	8	4
3	8	1	5	4	9	2	6	7

Page 72: Merry Matching

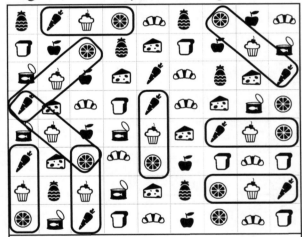

The sequence appears 9 times.

Page 74: Letters Y, H, E, F, W, A

whey	haw	we
yeah	yaw	he
awe	few	ha
hew	yew	*Other*
way	yea	*words are*
hey	aye	*possible.*

Pages 73-74: Challenge

1. Door	4. Pail	7. Rock
2. Fireplace	5. Fish	8. Tree
3. Jacket	6. Hose	

Page 76: Complete It! Weather

1. Rainy	6. Cloud
2. Caution	7. New
3. Storm	8. Head
4. Silver	9. Blowing
5. Check	10. Shine

Pages 77-78: Details

Page 79: Dif.

Pages 77-78: Details

Pages 81-82: Pictures

Pages 83-84: Silly

Sentence One:

D) Tom takes too many photos of the twisty tornado.

Sentence Two:

B) Kim counts clouds outside her extra wide window.

Pages 85: Odd One Out

Pages 86-87: Word Search, Summer Day

```
S J M G U H R B K C S U N N Y M A Q C G
N B E A C H N A I F X K X T R A V E L F
O I O A V O C A D C X V W L O O P I X Y
R A T H G I R B E I A D H H J K L G P W
K L B V H K N S I C A M J G W W Y N V P
E T R O P I C A L K O T P D N C V I O S
L V J F R D W C V Z O O E I T H A L W R
O I S F I I M G O L F H U O N T C I A P
V W C R C M O S K P V B E T M G A A U I
U I G P C U B C U S E M V S D C T S S C
L D Z A G H B Y L W L Y R K W O I Y U N
M E K R T E N O T I S D Y G J U O Z G I
S B I A N J C U C M Z J B M O X N R T C
F X O S K B A K T K U P D R D L V X S K
S L S O U U A Z T W A E K I H R P L I V
M B O L W R T H G I L Y A D L U E A D O
A I M W Q A E I F U V C T E U N F S M I
L K M C E C X L I K R L T A E H J G S S
S I M O U R L B O C E N Z B R C H A X W
L N U S Z E S Y N O L O Q S A R L T O T
A G Z H H V T E H M A V H V E Y J B S R
D W T S D F R G Y M X C M I L H T J O I
N L A Y M R O T Y A T Q D F C T W U D H
A E Y F H K H E Z H A K W M Q M N N P S
S Y E D J G S C J T H N V Z Z Q U J E T
```

Page 88: Sudoku

1	5	2	7	3	9	6	8	4
9	6	8	2	1	4	3	5	7
4	3	7	6	8	5	9	2	1
2	8	6	3	7	1	5	4	9
7	9	5	4	6	8	1	3	2
3	1	4	5	9	2	8	7	6
6	7	9	8	2	3	4	1	5
5	2	3	1	4	6	7	9	8
8	4	1	9	5	7	2	6	3

Pages 89-90: Challenge

1. Shelf
2. Curtain
3. Turtle
4. Bench
5. Pizza
6. Book
7. Leaf
8. Skirt

Page 90: E, G, R, L, D, I

glider	rile
ridge	ire
idler	gel
riled	dig
glide	lid
grid	rig
girl	led
dire	rid
lied	id
ride	*Other*
dreg	*words are*
gild	*possible.*

Page 92: Begins With 'S'

1. Subway
2. Skyscraper
3. Sydney[1]
4. Stadium
5. Shanghai[2]
6. Shopping
7. Stockholm[3]
8. Suburb

[1,2,3] Info source is Wikipedia in 2021

Page 95: Un.

1. Crowd
2. Store
3. Hotel
4. Noisy
5. Highway

Pages 93-94: Pictures

Page 96: Odd One Out

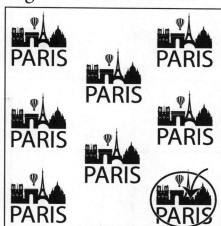

Pages 97-98: Lisa's List

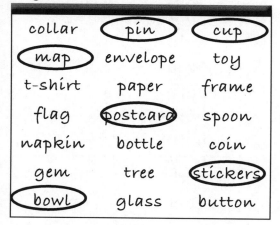

Pages 97-98: Dale's List

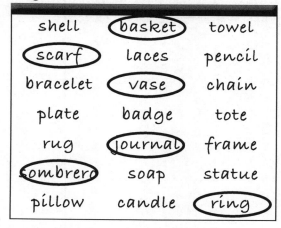

Page 100: Differences

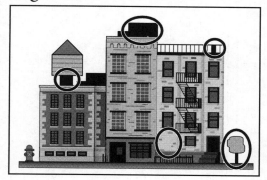

Pages 101-102: Silly Sentences

Sentence One:

C) Tanya takes the train to the merry museum.

Sentence Two:

B) Wally waddles to the super subway station.

Page 103: Sudoku

4	6	2	5	8	7	9	3	1
7	3	1	9	6	4	5	8	2
9	5	8	2	3	1	7	4	6
1	8	9	4	7	6	3	2	5
5	4	3	1	9	2	6	7	8
6	2	7	8	5	3	4	1	9
3	1	5	7	2	9	8	6	4
2	9	6	3	4	8	1	5	7
8	7	4	6	1	5	2	9	3

Page 106: Backwards

1. .ytic eht fo ygrene eht yojne I
2. .dnuora teg ot yaw tsaf a si yawbus ehT
3. .smuesum taerg sah ytiC kroY weN
4. .cifirret era nodnoL ni spohs ehT

Pages 107-108: Challenge

1. Sweater	5. Glasses
2. Chair	6. Phone
3. Squirrel	7. Cookie
4. Blanket	8. Pen

Pages 104-105: Word Search, Cities

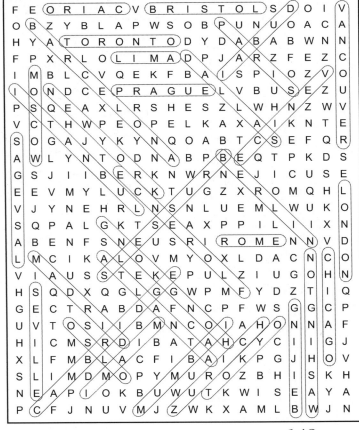

Page 108: R, P, V, T, E, I

rivet	pit
viper	tip
tripe	vet
pert	tie
pier	tip
tire	rep
rite	it
tier	*Other*
pet	*words are*
pie	*possible.*

Page 110: Odd One Out

Page 111: Begins With "B"

1. Bird watching
2. Board game
3. Book
4. Bowling
5. Baking
6. Beekeeping
7. Basketball
8. Billiards

Pages 113-114: Pictures

Page 112: Brainstorm

Coins, stamps, dolls, books, seashells, LPs, hats, DVDs, postcards, plates, cups, cards, buttons. *Many more possible.*

Page 112: Unscramble

1. Clay
2. Kiln
3. Glaze
4. Wheel
5. Ceramic

Page 116: Backwards

1. .tegdirB rof gnixaler si gnittinK
2. .yadretsey epacsdnal a detniap egroeG
3. .stop yalc lufituaeb stplucs neraK
4. .spuorg ni od ot nuf si gnitliuQ

Pages 117-118: Details

Answers

Page 119: Rhyme Time

Rhymes with "Game"

Name, same, brain, frame, grain, lame, blame, shame, flame, claim, fame, dame, aim, exclaim. *Other answers are possible.*

Rhymes with "Read"

Seed, feed, deed, bead, knead, reed, stead, weed, tweed, speed, peed, bleed, freed, lead, greed. *Other answers are possible.*

Pages 120-121: Coin Collecting

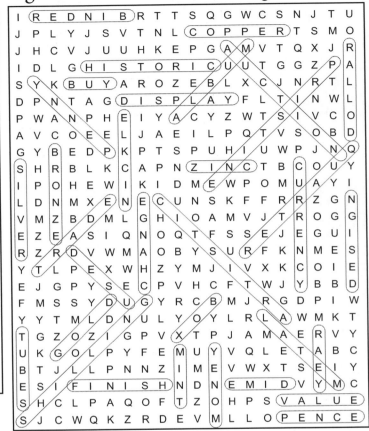

Page 122: Two of a Kind

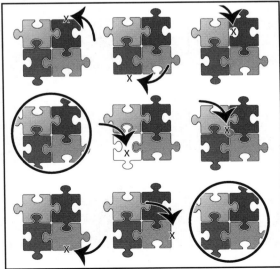

Pages 123-124: Kelly

easel   paper   *pencil*

pens   markers   palette

brush   panel   fabric

bowl   box   canvas

towel   spoon   knife

tape   chair   tote

stickers   apron   paint

Pages 123-124: Justin

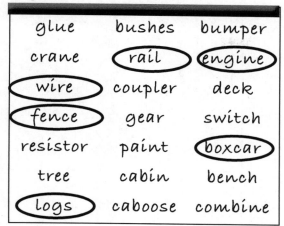

glue	bushes	bumper
crane	(rail)	(engine)
(wire)	coupler	deck
(fence)	gear	switch
resistor	paint	(boxcar)
tree	cabin	bench
(logs)	caboose	combine

Pages 125-126: Challenge

1. Book	5. Fence
2. Socks	6. Lamp
3. Duck	7. Pool
4. Mirror	8. Shovel

Page 126: Pictures to Sayings

Barking up the wrong tree.

Page 128: Brainstorm

Poodle, labrador, bulldog, terrier, sheep dog, collie, hound, cocker spaniel, great dane, golden retriever, pug. *Many more possible.*

Pages 129-130: Details

Page 128: Unscramble

1. Cake	4. Cookie
2. Tart	5. Trifle
3. Fudge	

Page 131: Complete It!

1. Try	4. Policy	7. Acorns	10. Well
2. Reap	5. Present	8. Around	
3. Light	6. Will	9. Bold	

Pages 132-133: Musical Instruments

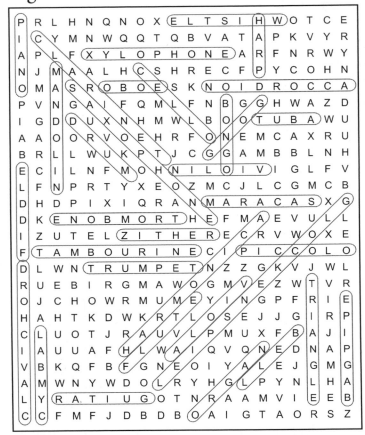

Page 134: Differences

— The End —

Thank you for using this book!

If you enjoyed this book, you may also enjoy the book to the right.

For more information check out the website:

www.LomicBooks.com

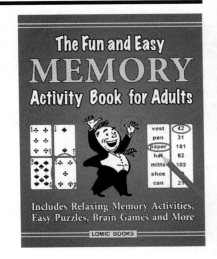

Made in the USA
Coppell, TX
30 December 2024